Life and Times

Florence Nightingale

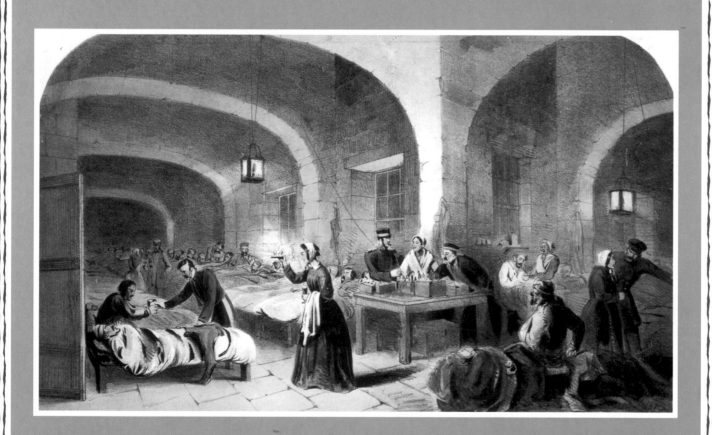

Peggy Burns

WAYLAND

Titles in the Life and Times series:

Florence Nightingale · Queen Elizabeth I ·
Queen Victoria · William Shakespeare ·

First published by Wayland Publishers Ltd, 61 Western Road, Hove, East Sussex BN3 1JD

Copyright © 1998 Wayland Publishers Ltd

British Library in Cataloguing Data
Burns, Peggy
  1. Nightingale, Florence – 1820 - 1910 – Juvenile literature
  2. Nurse administrators – Great Britain – Biography – Juvenile literature
  3. Crimean War – 1853 - 1856 – Participation – Female – Juvenile literature
  I. Title

610.7'3' 092

ISBN 0 7502 2291 3

Typeset in England by Joyce Chester
Printed and bound in Italy by
G. Canale & C.S.p.A, Turin

Editor: Carron Brown/Elizabeth Gogerly
Consultants: Norah Granger/
Alex Attewell of Florence Nightingale Museum
Cover designer: Jan Sterling
Text designer: Joyce Chester

Picture acknowledgements

The publishers gratefully acknowledge the following for allowing their pictures to be reproduced in this book: Billie Love 4 (left), 10, 15, 19 (right)/ Florence Nightingale Museum *title page*, 7, 12, 17, 18/19, 21, 22, 25, 26, 27 (top and bottom), 28/ Hulton Getty 13, 16/ Mary Evans Picture Library *cover* (background and main picture), 4 (right), 6, 11, 14, 18, 20, 23 (bottom), 24/ Oxford Scientific 21/ Peter Newark 9/ Wayland Picture Library 5, 23 (top), 29/ Wellcome Institute for the History of Medicine 8.

Find Wayland on the Internet at http://www.wayland.co.uk

All Wayland books encourage children to read and help them improve their literacy.

✓ The contents page, page numbers, headings and index help locate specific pieces of information.

✓ The glossary reinforces alphabetic knowledge and extends vocabulary.

✓ The further information section suggests other books dealing with the same subject.

✓ Find out more about how this book is specifically relevant to the National Literacy Strategy on page 31.

Contents

Dirty hospitals

'No Florence, you may not be a nurse!'

'But Mama…'

'I said no!'

Mrs Nightingale was very angry. She did not want her daughter to be a nurse.

Sick people queued outside this London hospital to see a doctor. ▼

Florence Nightingale as a young girl. ▶

▲ In the dirty and crowded cities poor people were often ill.

In Victorian times nurses knew very little about illness. They were usually rough and dirty women. Hospitals were filthy, smelly places.

In those days it was hard for poor people to be clean. Houses were crowded together. Several families shared one outside toilet. Only rich families like the Nightingales had bathrooms.

In 1824, nobody knew that germs existed. Germs grow in dirty places and cause disease. Germs are carried in the air, and on people's hands and clothes.

Life in a rich family

Rich young Victorian ladies usually spent their time reading, drawing pictures, playing the piano and going to parties. Sometimes they travelled, but few people had holidays abroad.

◀ Young ladies went to dances to meet rich husbands who would be able to look after them.

As a young girl, Florence Nightingale travelled through France and Italy with her parents and her older sister Parthenope. Her parents had also visited Italy when Florence was born. She was born in the city of Florence in 1820. Her parents decided to name her Florence after the beautiful city.

As a child Florence collected shells. All these things belonged to her. ▼

The quarrel

Even as a young girl Florence wanted to be a nurse. But at that time young ladies had to do what their parents told them. Mr and Mrs Nightingale wanted Florence to marry a rich gentleman. But Florence knew that she wanted to help other people and care for the sick.

Florence Nightingale, sitting down, with her sister Parthenope. ▶

They quarrelled about it. But Florence would not change her mind. In secret, she read a lot of books about medicine. She learned all she could about nursing.

A women's ward in the Middlesex Hospital, London, in 1808. ▼

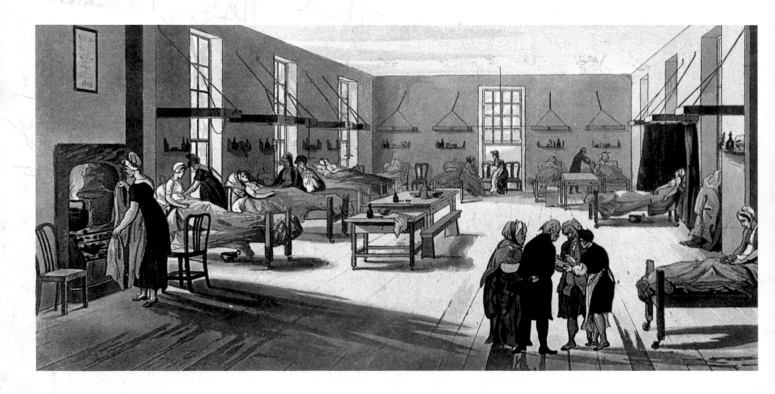

Learning to be a nurse

▲ Florence enjoyed her visits to Lea Hurst.

The Nightingales owned a house in Lea Hurst in Derbyshire. Florence sometimes stayed there and visited sick people in the village. She still wanted to be a nurse in a hospital. But Mr and Mrs Nightingale would not allow it.

Florence visited Paris and Germany and helped at hospitals there. Unfortunately, when she got home, her father, sister and grandmother became ill, one after another. So Florence spent the next two years nursing them all.

▲ Florence loved her pet owl, Athena.

Britain goes to war

In 1854, the Crimean War started between Russia and Turkey. Britain and France joined Turkey to fight against Russia.

▲ The battlefield. Big guns fired on the soldiers and horses.

▲ Officers and men relaxed during a break in the fighting. Life was hard for the men in such dirty conditions.

Thousands of British soldiers were killed or wounded. Many of the injured were taken to hospital at Scutari in Turkey.

At the hospital there was a shortage of doctors, medicines and bandages. Sometimes the men were left for a week without having their wounds bandaged.

Germs spread sickness

▲ Doctors and nurses treated the injured soldiers at a battlefield hospital.

In the hospital, sick and injured soldiers lay in dirty sheets still wearing their filthy clothes. Their bodies were covered in lice and fleas. The smell was terrible. Germs grew and spread diseases throughout the dirty hospital.

The doctors also spread disease by using dirty knives to operate on the men. More men died from disease than from their wounds. Back in England people read about the terrible state of the hospital in *The Times* newspaper.

British doctors went to the Crimea to help the soldiers. ▶

The new nurses

Florence Nightingale heard terrible stories too. She felt sorry for the wounded soldiers and offered to go to Scutari to help the men. She was asked to choose a group of women to take with her.

▲ Queen Victoria and her family visited wounded soldiers in hospital in Britain.

▲ Florence's pen and ink. This watch was her gift to a favourite cousin before she went to Scutari. The box lid shows Florence and her nurses on their way to Scutari.

Florence found thirty-eight women who wanted to come with her. Most of them had never nursed sick soldiers before. Florence Nightingale was put in charge of them.

Florence is not wanted

When Florence reached Scutari, she soon realised that some of the army officers and doctors did not want her help. The doctors were too busy to look after the hundreds of wounded soldiers. But they still did not want Florence and her nurses to help them.

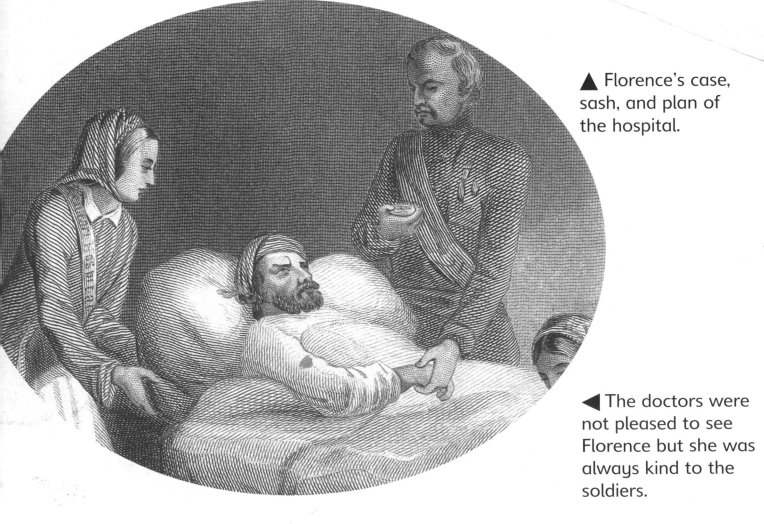

▲ Florence's case, sash, and plan of the hospital.

◀ The doctors were not pleased to see Florence but she was always kind to the soldiers.

Not much was known about germs in those days, but Florence believed in keeping things clean. She decided to clean up the hospital.

In Victorian times, it was thought that women were not as clever as men. They believed that women were only able to do jobs such as cooking and cleaning.

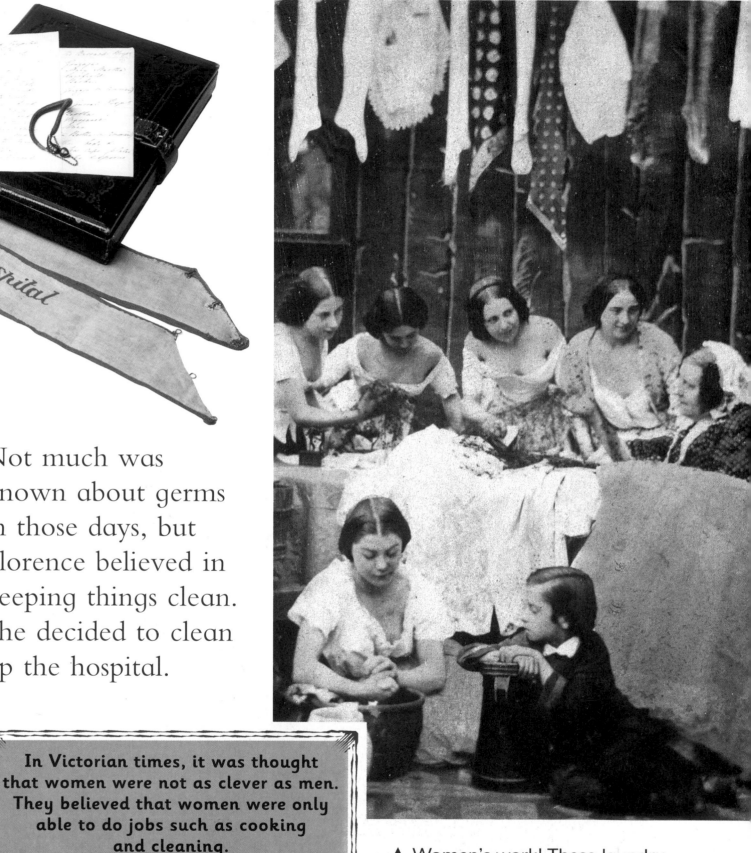

▲ Women's work! These laundry workers are washing clothes.

Cleaning up the hospital

The drains were blocked and the toilets were flowing over. The drinking water was dirty and rats ran around the filthy rooms. The hospital was in a horrible mess. But there was nothing to clean it with. That didn't stop Florence.

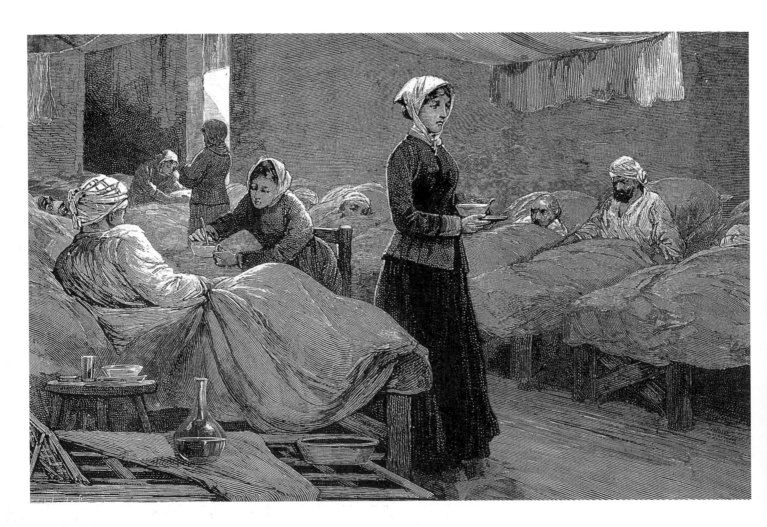

▲ Florence and her nurses cooked food and helped the sick men to eat.

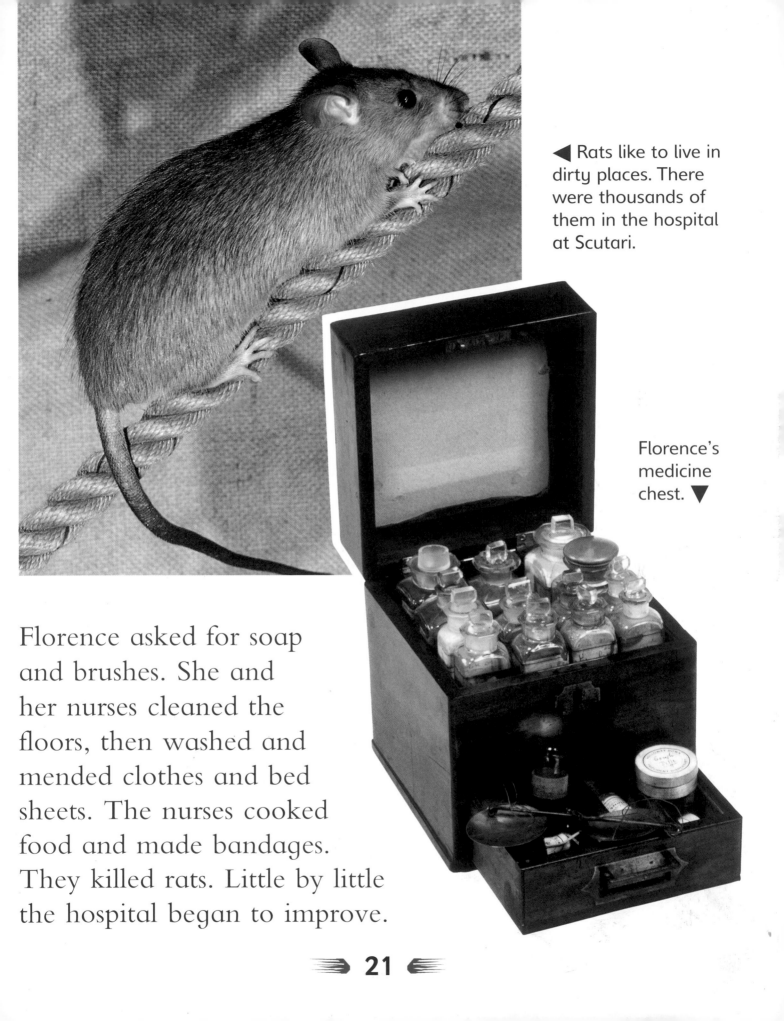

Rats like to live in dirty places. There were thousands of them in the hospital at Scutari.

Florence's medicine chest. ▼

Florence asked for soap and brushes. She and her nurses cleaned the floors, then washed and mended clothes and bed sheets. The nurses cooked food and made bandages. They killed rats. Little by little the hospital began to improve.

The lady with the lamp

Late at night, Florence would walk around the hospital with her lamp in her hand. She became known as the lady with the lamp.

▲ The lamp used by Florence.

That winter in Scutari it was bitterly cold. Thousands of men got sick and the hospital became very crowded. At last, the doctors asked Florence and her nurses to help them care for the men.

The women fed and washed the patients and bandaged their wounds. Florence joked with them to cheer them up. Sometimes, when a man was badly hurt, Florence held his hand until he died. The sick men became very fond of Florence.

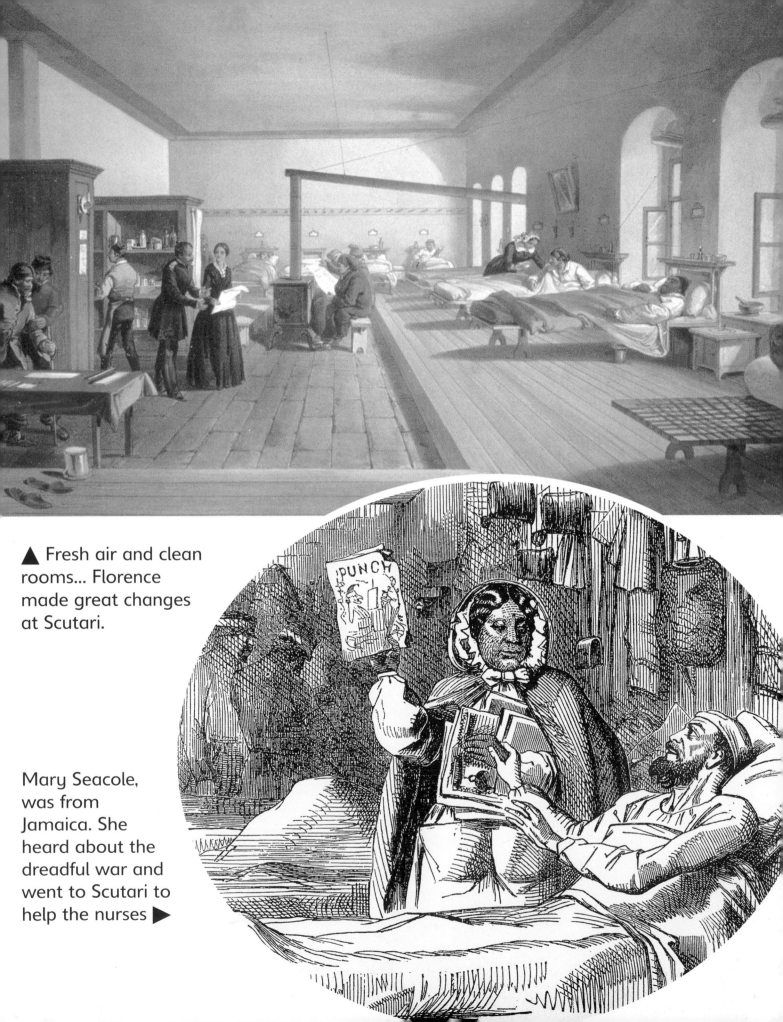

▲ Fresh air and clean rooms... Florence made great changes at Scutari.

Mary Seacole, was from Jamaica. She heard about the dreadful war and went to Scutari to help the nurses ▶

Florence becomes famous

Soon, Florence herself became very ill. Doctors did not think she would live. But she recovered and was able to nurse the soldiers again.

Florence after her return to England. ▶

When Florence was famous models of her became popular. ▼

In England, Florence Nightingale became well known for her good work. When the war was over, she went home to England. She was surprised to find that she had become famous.

But Florence was very sad about the soldiers who had died in the filthy army hospital. She wanted to help soldiers and other sick people in the future.

The Nightingale nurses

Florence Nightingale wrote many letters
to members of the government about the
state of the army hospitals. Things slowly
began to improve.

▲ Nightingale nurses were well trained. Florence in middle
age is pictured with her nurses.

Florence believed that if nurses were taught how to care for sick people, then hospitals everywhere would get better. She opened a school in London to teach young women how to nurse.

For the very first time, nurses were shown how to look after ill people. At last, everybody began to change their minds about nurses.

▲ A nurse's uniform from 1896.

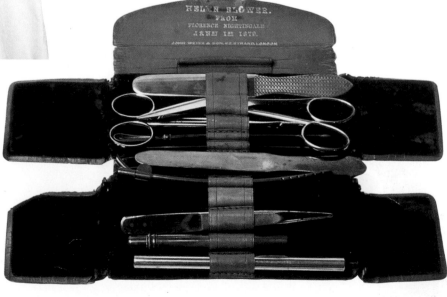

A case of nurse's instruments from Victorian times. ▶

Safe hospitals

When Florence was forty years old, she became ill again. She could not go out and had to rest in bed or on her sofa. But Florence kept on working and made plans for her school for nurses.

Florence Nightingale was ninety years old when she died in 1910.

Now, both men and women can train as nurses. It takes several years to learn how to be a nurse. But it is due to Florence Nightingale that nurses today are well trained and hospitals are safe for us all.

Clean and safe – care in hospitals today. ▼

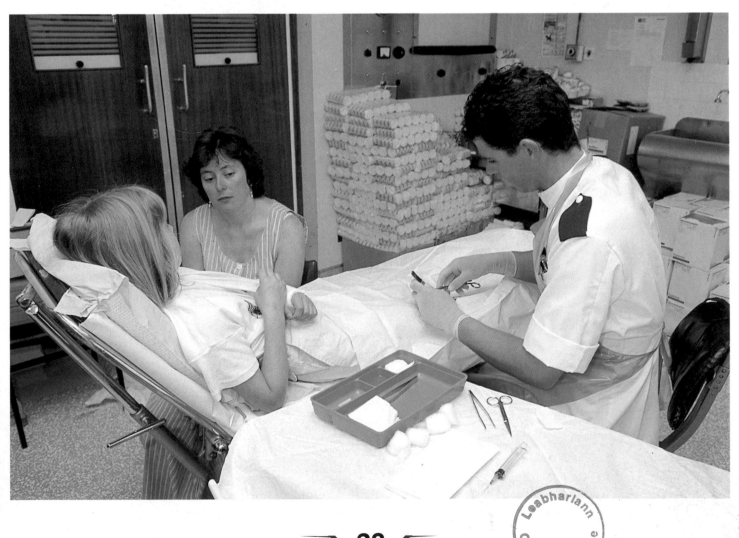

Timeline

1820 Florence Nightingale is born in Florence, Italy.

1854 Florence takes a group of women to the army hospital in Scutari, Turkey, to nurse the sick and wounded soldiers.

1855 Florence becomes very ill but recovers.

1856 The Crimean War ends. Florence returns to England.

1859 The Nightingale Training School for Nurses opens in London.

1910 Florence Nightingale dies.

Glossary

Bandages Strips of material used to bind up wounds.

Disease Illness.

Drains Pipes that take away waste water from sinks and toilets.

Fleas Insects which live and feed on animals or humans.

Germs Tiny living things. Some germs cause illness.

Government People who control a country.

Improve Make things better.

Injured Badly hurt.

Lice Tiny insects that can live on hair and skin.

Trained Taught how to do things properly at a college or school.

Ward A room for sick people in hospital.

Further information

Books to read

Famous People, Famous Lives – Florence Nightingale by Emma Fischel (Franklin Watts, 1997)

Tom's Lady of the Lamp by Jeanne Willis, illustrated by Amy Burch (Macdonald Young, 1995)

Two Lives – Florence Nightingale and Mary Seacole by Eric L. Huntley (Bogle L'Ouverture Press Ltd, 1993)

For advanced readers:

Coming Alive – Please Help Miss Nightingale by Stewart Ross (Evans Brothers Ltd, 1997)

Life Stories – Florence Nightingale by Nina Morgan (Wayland, 1995)

Places to visit

The Florence Nightingale Museum, Gassiot House, 2 Lambeth Palace Road, London SE1 7EW. Tel: 0171 620 0374

Use this book for teaching literacy

This book can help you in the literacy hour in the following ways:

✓ Children can re-tell the story of Florence Nightingale to give the main points in sequence and pick out significant incidents.

✓ Teaches children the stories behind part of our heritage, including the words we use.

✓ Children can use the story of Florence Nightingale and her times to write fictionalised accounts of, for example, Nightingale's role in the Crimean War.

Index

Numbers in **bold**
refer to pictures
as well as text.